Unsolved Mysteries W9-AKU-815

Giant Humanlike Beasts

Brian Innes

RSVP
RAINTREE
STECK-VAUGHN
P U B L I S H E R S
A Steck-Vaughn Company

Austin, Texas

Developed by Brown Partworks
Editor: Lindsey Lowe
Designer: Joan Curtis
Picture Researcher: Brigitte Arora

Raintree Steck-Vaughn Publishers Staff
Project Manager: Joyce Spicer
Editor: Pam Wells

Library of Congress Cataloging-in-Publication Data
Innes, Brian.
 Giant humanlike beasts/by Brian Innes.
  p. cm.—(Unsolved mysteries)
 Includes bibliographical references and index.
 ISBN 0-8172-5484-6 (Hardcover)
 ISBN 0-8172-5846-9 (Softcover)
 1. Yeti—Juvenile literature. 2. Sasquatch—Juvenile literature.
 3. Wild men—Juvenile literature.
 I. Title. II. Series: Innes, Brian. Unsolved mysteries.
 QL89.2.Y4I56 1999
 001.944—dc21   98-28736
                                                CIP
                                                AC
Printed and bound in the United States
1 2 3 4 5 6 7 8 9 0 WZ 02 01 00 99 98

Acknowledgments

Cover Galen Rowell/Corbis; **Page 5:** Christine
Kolisch/Corbis; **Page 6:** Ivan T. Sanderson/Fortean
Picture Library; **Page 7:** Keren Su/Corbis; **Page 9:**
Eric Shipton and Michael Ward/Mary Evans Picture
Library; **Page 10:** John Cleare; **Page 11:** Hulton-
Deutsch Collection/Corbis; **Page 13:** Michael S.
Yamashita/Corbis; **Page 14:** Fortean Picture Library;
Page 15: Dr. Zhou Guoxing/Fortean Picture Library;
Page 16: International Society of Cryptozoology;
Page 17: Natural History Museum, London; **Page 19:**
Bridgeman Art Library; **Page 20:** George Lepp/Corbis;
Page 21: Keren Su/Corbis; **Page 23:** Rene Dahinden
/Fortean Picture Library; **Page 24:** UPI/Corbis-
Bettmann; **Page 25:** Fortean Picture Library;
Page 27: Patterson/Gimlin © 1968, Rene
Dahinden/Fortean Picture Library; **Page 28:** Fortean
Picture Library; **Page 29:** Gunter Marx/Corbis;
Pages 30, 32, 33, 34: Rene Dahinden/Fortean Picture
Library; **Page 35:** Popperfoto; **Page 37:** Loren
Coleman/Fortean Picture Library; **Page 38:** Fortean
Picture Library; **Page 41:** Natural History Museum,
London; **Page 43:** Wolfgang Kaehler/Corbis;
Page 44: Popperfoto; **Page 45:** Fortean Picture
Library; **Page 46:** Cliff Crook/Fortean Picture Library.

Contents

Abominable Snowman

Somewhere in the cold Himalaya Mountains lives a giant beast. It is known as the Abominable Snowman.

Every year, groups of climbers and their local guides begin to climb the mountains of the Himalayas (opposite). Many have found mysterious trails of footprints in the smooth, white snow.

The Himalaya Mountains stretch for more than 1,500 miles (2,413.5 km) along the northern border of India. In spring, 1925, photographer N. A. Tombazi was with a group of climbers in the Himalayas. They had reached the Zemu Glacier, at a height of 15,000 feet (4,575 m). Apart from a few small bushes, snow stretched all around them. Suddenly one of the local guides stopped. He pointed to a spot about 300 yards (274 m) away.

At first Tombazi could see nothing. He was blinded by the sun shining off the snow. Then he spotted a figure. It was walking upright, stopping every now and then to pull at the bushes. Tombazi said: "It showed up dark against the snow and, as far as I could make out, wore no clothes. Within the next minute or so it had moved into some thick scrub. . . ." It could not be seen in the bushes and shrubs.

"A couple of hours later, I purposely made a detour [changed direction], so as to pass the place where the 'man' or 'beast' had been seen. I examined the footprints, which were clearly visible on the surface of the snow. They were similar in shape to those of a man."

4

People call the Himalaya Mountains "the roof of the world." The highest point is Mount Everest. . . .

Tombazi was a member of the British Royal Geographical Society. This is a scientific organization that is respected worldwide. He was certainly somebody to be trusted. He had no doubt that he had seen the creature known locally as the "yeti."

HOME OF THE YETI

People call the Himalaya Mountains "the roof of the world." At 15,000 feet (4,575 m), there is snow all year round—the word "Himalaya" actually means "home of the snows." There are some 96 peaks at a height of over 24,000 feet (7,320 m), but the highest point is Mount Everest, at 29,028 feet (8,848 m).

Mount Everest stands right on the border between China and Nepal. Nepal is a small country in the Himalayas that lies between northern India and China. The people who live on the lower slopes of Mount Everest are called Sherpas. They believe that there are two kinds of creatures living among the high snows. The Sherpas call one of them *dzu-teh*. Experts think that this is probably the common Himalayan black bear. The other is the *yeh-teh*, or yeti.

The Sherpas describe the yeti as being about the size of a human. They say it has a pointed head and walks upright on two legs. It has long arms and is covered with reddish hair. The yeti is said to live in the area where the trees stop and the high snows begin. Sometimes it

This is a drawing of what a Himalayan yeti, or "snowman," might look like.

6

This Tibetan farmer is using a couple of yaks to pull his plow. Some farmers have reported that their yaks have been killed by yetis in search of food.

moves down the mountainside to steal food from villages. It may also kill yaks—large, hairy oxen that the farmers keep for milk, plowing, and clothing.

The first report of a yeti sighting by a European came from a British major, L. A. Waddell, in 1889. He found large humanlike footprints in the snow while climbing on Everest at a height of 17,000 feet (5,185 m). He wrote that some claimed these prints were "the trail of the hairy wild man believed to live among the eternal [everlasting] snows." But Waddell decided that they were likely to be the tracks of a bear. For more than 30 years, nobody paid much attention to his report. Then the yeti gained a new name that made it world famous.

HUNT FOR THE SNOWMAN

In 1921 a man named Kenneth Howard–Bury was leading a British expedition to Mount Everest. At around 20,000 feet (6,100 m), he and his team saw

7

dark figures moving across the snow above them. When they reached the spot, they found a series of giant footprints. The Sherpa guides said they must have been made by *metoh-kangmi*. This was a term or nickname that the Sherpas used to describe any unknown mountain animal. When Howard–Bury reported his sighting, the nickname was translated, or put into English, as the "Abominable Snowman."

A huge yeti, nearly 9 feet (3 m) tall, picked him up and carried him to a cave.

The name caught the attention of newspaper editors all over the world. At the time, there were many mountaineers, or people who climb mountains, who wanted to be the first to reach the very top of Mount Everest. Now they had an additional purpose—to find the Abominable Snowman.

TALL TALES?

In 1938, Captain d'Auvergne told an amazing story. He said he had been traveling alone in the Himalayas. He was exhausted and nearly blinded by the snow. A huge yeti, nearly 9 feet (3 m) tall, picked him up and carried him to a cave. There the creature fed and looked after him until he was able to walk again.

The next sighting was made in 1942. Slavomir Rawicz was a Pole. He had been captured by the Russians during World War II, but he and six others had escaped from their prison camp. They had walked 2,000 miles (3,218 km) to freedom, crossing the Himalayas into India. On the way they met two huge yeti: "They were nearly 8 feet [2.5 m] tall . . . The heads were squarish [square-shaped]. The shoulders sloped sharply down to a powerful chest and long arms, the wrists of which reached the knees."

Rawicz said he and his companions watched the creatures for two hours. One was slightly larger than the other, and Rawicz guessed they were male and female. They did not seem interested in the humans.

In 1951, British climbers Eric Shipton and Michael Ward were walking on Mount Everest when they found a set of tracks. They followed them for nearly a mile. One footprint was very clear. They took photographs of it. Ward put his ice ax beside it to give an idea of the size. This proved the footprint was nearly 13 inches (33 cm) long and 8 inches (20 cm) wide.

This is a photograph of one of the footprints that Eric Shipton and Michael Ward found in the Himalayas in 1951. The print was 13 inches (33 cm) long.

This Tibetan man is holding what was said to be the scalp of a yeti. However, an expert said it was made from goat skin.

Describing his experience later, Eric Shipton wrote: "There could be no doubt whatever that a large creature had passed that way a very short time before. Whatever it was, it was not a human being, not a bear, not any species of monkey known to exist in Asia." The footprint had five toes. The two inner toes were longer than the rest. The heel was very broad and flat.

The photographs were looked at by a group of scientists who study animals. They said that they thought the tracks might have been made by a bear, or by some type of large monkey. Nevertheless Shipton, and many other people, refused to believe the prints had been made by animals.

ON TOP OF THE WORLD

Two years later New Zealander Edmund Hillary and Sherpa Tenzing Norgay were the first men to stand on the top of Mount Everest. But the news of their success was almost forgotten when they reported that they, too, had seen the tracks of the yeti. Tenzing said he had often seen similar tracks. He told Hillary that his father had once been chased down a steep slope by one of the creatures.

10

A London newspaper, the *Daily Mail*, organized its own Abominable Snowman Expedition in 1954. It had little success, however. A reporter named Ralph Izzard led the expedition. The team only found a few tracks in the snow. They also photographed what was said to be the scalp of a yeti, which they found in a Tibetan monastery. A monastery is a building where monks live. In 1961, Edmund Hillary borrowed the scalp and took it to be examined by experts. They announced that it was made from the skin of a wild goat that lived in the area!

Many people have seen Abominable Snowman footprints like these in the snows of the Himalayas. Some have photographed them. However, nobody has yet photographed the creature itself—if it exists!

THE MYSTERY LIVES ON

In recent years, after the excitement of the 1950s, less has been heard about the Abominable Snowman. However, reports are still being made today. Some unknown creature surely exists high in the Himalaya Mountains, leaving footprints in the snow and scaring the local Sherpas.

Interestingly, reports of such a creature do not come only from this area. There are also stories of the Wildman deep in the forests of China; creatures called the Almas in central Asia; the Bigfoot in North America; and many other strange humanlike beasts.

Wildman of China

There are many tales of a large, humanlike creature living in the wild forests of the Chinese mountains.

One evening early in 1976, some Chinese loggers were traveling in their truck down a dirt road through the forest. They had been working high in the mountains of Hubei Province. This is a wild area 600 miles (965 km) up the valley of the great Chang (Yangtze) River. There are huge, thick forests, almost unexplored, and few roads or villages.

Suddenly the headlights of the truck showed a large, hairy figure. It was standing in the middle of the dirt road. The driver braked quickly, and several men got down. They approached to within just a few yards of the creature. Then it turned and disappeared into the undergrowth.

A CHINESE LEGEND

The men were sure it was not a bear. And it was not any other forest animal they had seen before. They decided that it must have been a "Wildman." Tales of the Wildman have been told by the Chinese for many centuries. Like the Abominable Snowman of the Himalaya Mountains, the Wildman is said to be tall, heavily built, and covered with hair. The men sent a report to the Chinese Academy of Sciences.

The valley of the Chang (Yangtze) River is bordered by thick forests (opposite). Most of these are unexplored. Many people think they are home to the Wildman of China.

The men were sure
it was not a bear. . . .
They decided
that it must
have been a
"Wildman."

For a long time experts did not believe these stories. But then, in 1950, a scientist named Fan Jingquan reported that he had sighted two creatures in a forest in Shanxi Province.

Other sightings began to be reported. In 1961, men were building a road through a thick forest in the Yunnan Province. They claimed that they had killed a young female Wildman. They said that it was only about 4 feet (1.2 m) tall. The Chinese Academy of Sciences immediately sent a team of experts to the area, but they could find no trace of the body. They decided it must have been a monkey.

The Wildman is said to be large and covered with thick hair, as shown in the drawing on this Chinese poster. The writing says, "Have you seen the Wildman?"

COLLECTING PROOF

After the 1976 sighting in Hubei Province, there were many more reports, all from the same region, or area. The Chinese government decided to see if they could find any proof that the creature existed. A scientific team was put together by Zhou Guoxing, a professor at the Natural History Museum in Beijing. There were nearly 100 experts in the group. They were helped by several units from the Chinese Army.

Over a period of two years, the scientific team carefully searched through the thick forests of Hubei Province. They covered an area of some 500 square miles (1,295 sq km) and gathered dozens of descriptions from local people.

One report was particularly interesting. In June 1976, a woman named Gong Yulan said that she had seen a hairy, humanlike creature. It was scratching its back against a tree. She showed the scientists the tree, and they found hairs trapped in the bark. The hairs were sent back to be examined in Beijing. Experts reported that they came from an unknown animal. It was an apelike creature. But the hairs did not match those from any known species.

FACE-TO-FACE

The most amazing story was told by Pang Gensheng. He was a team leader from a local commune, or rural community. He said that he had been out chopping wood when he met a Wildman.

The creature had walked toward him. Terrified, Gensheng backed away until he found himself up against the bottom of a cliff. He had nowhere to go. The Wildman approached. Gensheng raised his ax to

Gong Yulan (at center) talking to Dr. Zhou Guoxing and a group of Chinese soldiers. She claimed to have seen a Wildman by this tree on June 19, 1976.

15

protect himself, and the creature stopped. Gensheng said he and the Wildman stood looking at each other for nearly an hour. Then he reached down and picked up a large rock. He threw it and hit the beast in the chest. It howled and then ran a short distance away. Afterward it stopped and leaned against a tree before running off. Gensheng said the Wildman had been about 7 feet (2 m) tall. He said it had wide shoulders, a sloping forehead, and long arms.

These were just two reports of the sightings in Hubei Province. The members of the scientific expedition were very excited. But they were unable to spot a Wildman for themselves. However, they did find huge footprints and several individual hairs.

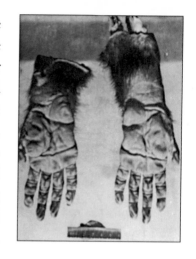

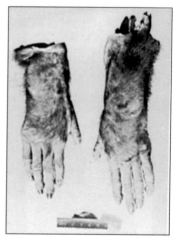

GIANT APES

Dr. Guoxing was just one of many scientists who were convinced that the animal existed. In 1980 he was sent some preserved hands and feet. They were said to have been taken from a

Dr. Guoxing photographed the "Wildman hands" sent to him in 1980 (top and above). The 6-inch (15 cm) rule shows their size.

dead Wildman. However, when Guoxing looked at them carefully, he decided that they came from a type of monkey. This could explain the small "Wildman" killed by the road builders in Yunnan Province.

As an expert on prehistoric beings, Guoxing knew all about the large *Gigantopithecus* ape species that has died out. In 1935 a German scientist, G. H. R. von

Koenigswald, had bought some large teeth from a Chinese druggist in Hong Kong. Koenigswald was an anthropologist, an expert on the beginnings, development, and customs of humans. He believed that the teeth were from a huge, humanlike creature.

Twenty years later a Chinese anthropologist, Pei Wen Xung, proved that they had, in fact, come from a huge ape that had lived in China until about a million years ago. Because of its size the creature was called *Gigantopithecus*, meaning "giant ape." It was said to be bigger than a large gorilla—around 12 feet (4 m) tall and close to 690 pounds (313 kg). Dr. Guoxing wondered if these apes could still be living in China after all. He pointed out that other ancient species are still with us today. These include the tapir, which is a large animal with hoofs that looks something like a pig, and the giant panda. Both species of animals are found in China.

A LIVING WILDMAN?

There are still many creatures to be discovered in the unexplored parts of the world. Does *Gigantopithecus* still live deep in the Chinese forests? Or perhaps the Wildman is an even closer but unknown relative of modern humans.

This drawing shows an adult Gigantopithecus and its baby. Perhaps this creature is the real "Wildman" of China.

17

The Asian Almas

The lands of central Asia cover a large area of the world. It is possible that wild people roam its most distant parts.

Early in the 15th century, Hans Schiltberger, a Bavarian soldier from southern Germany, was captured by the Turks. He was treated as a slave, and after a while was sold to a Mongol prince. The prince's name was Timur (Tamerlane), and although Schiltberger was still a slave, he became one of the prince's advisors. Working for Prince Timur, Schiltberger traveled throughout central Asia. However, he finally managed to escape and find his way back home to Europe.

A GREAT ADVENTURE

In 1430, Schiltberger wrote an account of his adventures. He described some of the many wild creatures that he had seen on his travels through Asia: "In the mountains live wild people who have nothing in common with other humans. Only the hands and face are free of hair. They run around in the hills like animals, and eat foliage [the leaves of a tree or plant] and grass, and whatever else they can find. The lord of the territory made . . . a present of a couple of forest people, a man and a woman. They had been caught in the wilderness, together with three untamed horses. . . ."

This picture shows Prince Timur with some of his advisors (opposite). While working for the prince, Schiltberger saw many amazing people and animals.

Working for Prince Timur, Schiltberger traveled throughout central Asia.

A female Przewalski's horse and her foal. Very few survive in their native Mongolia. These horses were photographed in a wildlife park in California.

More than four centuries later, in the 1870s, the Russian explorer Nikolai Przewalski discovered these wild Mongolian horses. The species has been named after him. It is now extremely rare, although a few horses are protected in wildlife parks. On the same expedition Przewalski also heard tales of "wild men," but unfortunately he was unable to discover any.

ANIMAL OR HUMAN?

One of the earliest descriptions of these "wild men" was written in Arabic in the 12th century. It describes a creature that was said to live on the plains of Turkestan. It said the creature stood upright on two legs, like a human. The writer of the description thought that this creature was nearly human.

In several Arabic languages this creature is called the Almas. This is what it is now called. During the 19th century other reports of the Almas began to be written. It seemed to be something like the Wildman

20

of China. It was said to be about the same height as humans, but covered with dark or reddish hair. It had long arms, and walked with the legs bent. The forehead sloped back from a bony ridge over the eyes. It had a large lower jaw, but not much chin. It had big feet, with wide, spoon-shaped toes, while its hands were humanlike, but with long fingers.

Around 1910 a Kazakh herdsman in west central Asia met with Russian zoologist V.A. Khaklov. The Kazakh said he had watched a female Almas for several weeks. She had been captured by some farmers. Later she was set free. The herdsman described how she behaved: "This creature was usually quite silent, but she screeched and bared her teeth on being

This Kazakh herdsman has rescued a sheep from the winter snow. Several herdsmen claimed to have seen Almas while rounding up their flocks.

approached. She had a peculiar way of lying down, or sleeping. She squatted on her knees and elbows, resting her forehead on the ground. Her hands were folded over the back of her head. She would eat only raw meat, some vegetables, and grain, and sometimes insects that she caught. When drinking water, she would lap in animal fashion, or sometimes dip her arm into the water and lick her fur."

" . . . he can pick up a chair, with a man sitting in it, with his teeth."

BORIS PORSHNEV

THE STORY OF ZANA

The strangest tale of all concerns a female Almas named Zana. She was captured somewhere in central Asia in the late 19th century. After some time she came into the hands of a Russian farmer named Edgi Genaba. At first, she was very wild and had to be watched night and day. After several years, however, she became tamer and was allowed to roam free.

Zana was large and very strong. Her skin was covered with reddish-black hair. She had a large jaw and big teeth, high cheekbones, and a flat nose. She never learned to talk, but muttered to herself. However, she could carry out jobs on her master's orders. When she was alone, she would spend hours banging and grinding stones together. She had her first child by a local villager. When it was born, she carried it to the river to wash it. But the baby could not stand the coldness of the water, and died. After that, the villagers took her children away from her when they were first born so that they could be looked after. It was said that Zana had two sons and two daughters that lived.

In 1964 a Russian scientist named Boris Porshnev visited the village. He wanted to collect what information he could about Zana. He was told that her youngest son, Khvit, had been a farmer. He was "extremely strong, difficult to deal with, and wild." Khvit seemed to be restless and uncontrollable.

LIVING RELATIONS

Porshnev also met two people who claimed they were Zana's grandchildren. From the time he saw them he was surprised by the way they looked. "Shalikula, the grandson, has unusually powerful jaw muscles, and he can pick up a chair, with a man sitting in it, with his teeth."

Over the next few years Professor Porshnev spent time in the overgrown village cemetery. He wanted to discover Zana's remains. He was not successful, but at last he found a skull, which he believed to be that of her youngest son Khvit. The skull had a very large, powerful lower jaw. Porshnev was convinced that it showed the features of a prehistoric human that was known as Neanderthal.

Professor Boris Porshnev in his study. He is holding the plaster cast of a giant footprint found in central Asia.

23

These Neanderthal skulls were part of a special show at the American Museum of Natural History in 1984. Porshnev believed the Almas were Neanderthals.

Boris Porshnev was also extremely interested in the reports of the way in which Zana had knocked and ground stones together. He wondered if this had been an attempt to make tools out of stone.

NEANDERTHAL SURVIVORS

Just before his death in 1974, Professor Porshnev published an article in the science magazine titled *Current Anthropology*. He suggested that the Almas is a survivor of the prehistoric Neanderthal people. This idea was supported by Professor John Napier, an expert on primate biology—that is, the study of the group of mammals that includes humans, apes, and monkeys. Napier wrote that he thought it was possible the Almas were the descendants of Neanderthals from the last ice age.

In 1925, Russian military surgeons had made a detailed examination of a body that was said to be a dead Almas. It was of medium height and heavily built. There were no great differences between its skeleton and that of modern humans. However, the head was different. It had a sloping forehead, and its brow stuck out. The lower jaw was huge, and it had a short nose. This was like the remains of prehistoric Neanderthal people that have been discovered.

HUNTING FOR THE ALMAS

In more recent years a scientist named Marie-Jeanne Koffman spent a long time collecting reports about the Almas. She collected dozens of stories from many people who claimed to have seen the creature in the Caucasus Mountains of southwest Russia.

In one, no less than 30 people told how they had seen an Almas eating corncobs in a field. Koffman's team found a line of footprints in the field and made plaster casts of the tracks. They also found two Almas caves that contained mounds of potatoes and fruits. Some had the marks of humanlike teeth on them. These marks showed that the teeth must have been set in a jaw slightly wider than most human jaws.

Scientist Igor Burtsev with a cast of a giant footprint that was found in 1979. Others are still being found.

Koffman believes that this creature still exists, but that human activity in the area is threatening its continued survival. It is almost certain that no living Almas have ever been found and saved, like Przewalski's horse was. Until a living creature is captured so that scientists can study it, we will never know the real truth about the Almas.

25

Bigfoot of North America

Perhaps the most famous of the giant humanlike beasts is Bigfoot. It is the only one said to have been filmed.

Roger Patterson showed experts the film he had made of Bigfoot in 1967 (opposite). Many people thought the film was real. Others, however, were not so sure.

On the afternoon of October 20, 1967, Roger Patterson and his friend Bob Gimlin were riding their horses through the wooded highlands of northern California, near the border with Oregon. They were headed northward alongside Bluff Creek, a shallow waterway that flows into the Klamath River.

Just ahead was a tangle of logs and fallen trees, about 15 feet (4.5 m) high. As the riders reached it, a huge hairy figure stood up on the other side of the creek. The horses snorted with fear, rearing and backing. Patterson was thrown from his saddle. The creature began to stride away.

CAUGHT ON FILM

Patterson had a small movie camera in his saddlebag. Quickly he yanked it out. Plunging through the wet sand, he began to film, trying to keep the camera aimed at the creature. It turned to look at him and then disappeared into the undergrowth. And, at the same moment, Patterson discovered that he had run out of film.

The horses had run away, and it took the two men nearly an hour to find them. When they returned to the creek, the creature was long

It turned to look at him and then disappeared into the undergrowth.

This is Roger Patterson holding two plaster casts of huge footprints. The photograph was taken within hours of his filming Bigfoot in October 1967.

gone. But there were footprints in the sand. Patterson and Gimlin were able to make plaster casts of them. They were 14½ inches (36.8 cm) long and 5 inches (12.7 cm) wide. The length of the creature's single step was some 40 inches (101.6 cm).

FEMALE BIGFOOT

When the film was developed, Patterson found he had about 24 feet (7.3 m) of footage. It ran for about a minute. It was jumpy and difficult to make out at first. But there was no doubt what it showed—a heavily built creature.

The creature was obviously a female. She had reddish-black hair all over her body, except for her lower face, the palms of her hands, and the soles of her feet. Her head seemed to grow right into her shoulders, without a neck. And her forehead sloped back to a high point at the back of her head.

She had thick arms, longer than a human's. Her legs were powerful. She walked with them bent. In fact, she looked something like a gorilla. Patterson and Gimlin claimed that they had taken the first moving pictures of the creature known in legends as Bigfoot.

SIGHTINGS OF BIGFOOT

Native Americans have told stories of "Bigfoot" (known as Sasquatch—"hairy giant"—in Canada) for centuries. Like the yeti, the Wildman, and the Almas, Bigfoot is tall, heavily built, and covered with reddish–black hair. It gets its popular name from the huge footprints that it leaves. Most sightings of the creature have been in the wild country of the northwestern United States, or across the border with Canada in

A thick forest in British Columbia, Canada. Most sightings of the Sasquatch have been reported in British Columbia.

29

British Columbia. In 1884 a British Columbia newspaper, the *Daily Colonist*, carried a story about the capture of one creature. The Sasquatch was spotted by the crew of a train, traveling between the towns of Lytton and Yale. They stopped the train and gave chase. The being they captured was built like a gorilla and covered with blackish hair. They called it Jacko. Jacko was put on show in the region, and then (it is said) was sold to the Barnum & Bailey Circus.

MEETING THE FAMILY

During the early 1900s more reports of sightings began to appear. Then, in 1924, a Canadian logger had an amazing experience. His name was Albert Ostman. He was worried that people would think he was crazy, so he didn't tell his story for 33 years. Then, on August 20, 1957, he took an oath, promising to tell the truth, before a court official at Fort Langley,

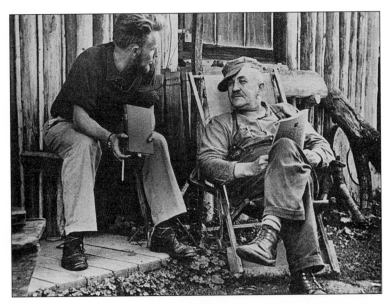

Albert Ostman (on the right) received many visits from journalists in 1957. In August of that year he told how a Bigfoot had taken him prisoner in 1924.

British Columbia. According to Ostman, he had been camping near the head of Toba Inlet, opposite Vancouver Island. One night he woke up to find himself being carried inside his sleeping bag "like a sack of potatoes. The only thing in sight was a huge hand, clutching the partly closed neck of the bag."

Patterson and Gimlin claimed that they had taken the first moving pictures of . . . Bigfoot.

When Ostman was finally dumped on the ground, he found himself in the middle of a family of four Bigfeet. He claimed that the father of the family was 8 feet (2.5 m) tall, and the mother was about 7 feet (2 m) tall. There was what appeared to be a "teenage" son and a younger daughter. During the day the females searched for food. They brought sweet grass, different roots, and the fresh tips of pine and spruce trees. Meanwhile, the male bigfeet kept watch on Albert Ostman. The logger said he was kept prisoner for six days before he managed to escape.

SEARCHING FOR BIGFOOT
Albert Ostman's story finally came out at a time when there was still great popular interest in Eric Shipton's photograph of yeti tracks in the Himalaya Mountains. The story caught the interest of a Canadian newspaper man named John Green. He joined forces with a Swiss-born Canadian named René Dahinden. The two men spent the best part of the next 30 years in search of Bigfoot.

CLOSE ENCOUNTER

In 1955, Dahinden had taken the statement of a trapper named William Roe. Roe had been exploring a deserted gold mine near Jasper, Alberta. There he saw a creature that, at first, he thought was a grizzly bear: "Then I saw it was not a bear. My first impression [understanding of what he saw] was of a huge man, about 6 feet [1.8 m] tall, almost 3 feet [0.9 m] wide, and probably weighing near 300 pounds [136 kg]. It was covered from head to foot with dark brown, silver-tipped hair." Roe watched the creature as it came closer. It squatted and began to strip leaves from some branches.

A TIMID BEAST

Suddenly the creature spotted Roe, who said: "A look of amazement crossed its face. Still in a crouched position, it backed up three or four steps, then straightened up to its full height." The trapper said he thought about shooting the beast. However, it was so humanlike that he was unable to raise his rifle. As it walked away, it made "a peculiar noise that seemed to be half laugh and half language."

René Dahinden beside a trail of giant footprints in California on August 29, 1967. Two months later, Patterson made his film of Bigfoot at Bluff Creek, just five miles (8 km) from where these footprints were found.

This is a strip of the film that Patterson shot of Bigfoot in 1967. Each picture is called a frame. These frames were studied by experts to see if the film was a trick.

In the fall of 1958, John Green went to the Bluff Creek region of northern California to check out a new report that he had received. A work crew was building a road through the area. One morning a bulldozer operator named Jerry Crew found huge footprints by his machine. For two months the work crew found more tracks circling their heavy equipment. Jerry made casts of one set of footprints. They were 2 inches (5 cm) deep and 16 inches (41 cm) long.

EXAMINING THE FILM

In August 1967 more footprints were found in the same area. Then, in October, Patterson shot his famous movie footage of Bigfoot there. The film was shown on television and seen by millions of people. Most scientific experts said it was a hoax, or trick—they said it was probably a man dressed in a gorilla suit.

Much of the discussion about whether the film was a trick or not centered around the speed at which it had been shot. The normal speed for movies is 24 frames per second (fps). A British expert, Donald W. Grieve, said

These Bigfoot footprints were found by a group of elk hunters on Coleman Ridge near Ellensburg, Washington State, on November 6, 1970.

that at this speed the creature appeared to move like a human. This would mean that the figure was probably a man in a gorilla suit. However, Grieve also went on to say that if the speed of Patterson's film had actually been set at 16 or 18 fps, then the creature must be real. At the slower film speed, said Grieve, it would be impossible for a human to move like the figure on the film. Roger Patterson was unable to remember the setting of his camera, but he thought it might have been running at 18 fps. Later, Russian scientists in Moscow tried a clever experiment. They measured the way the camera bobbed up and down as Patterson ran forward. At 24 fps, they said, he would have taken six strides per second. This is faster than a world-class sprinter. The experts decided the film must have been running at about 16 fps. Therefore, it was not a hoax.

NO ZIPPER!

Roger Patterson died in 1972, but the experts still continue to question whether the film was a trick or not. Shortly after Patterson's death, René Dahinden

34

took the film to the Walt Disney studios. Disney films are famous for their animated animal characters. They are experts in movie trickery. However, people at the Disney studios said they could not have created a hoax so well. If the figure was a human dressed as a gorilla, nobody has yet discovered what film people call "the zipper in the suit."

OTHER SIGHTINGS

Between June 1964 and December 1970 alone, 25 separate Bigfoot sightings were reported. The total number of reported accounts of giant footprints and living creatures now runs into thousands.

During the late 1960s, John Napier was a professor in Washington, D.C. Later, he worked at the University of London. In early 1972 he published a book about Bigfoot. In it he said: "No one doubts that some of the footprints are hoaxes. . . ." However, he also went on to say that if any one of the reports turned out to be true, then the matter would have to be taken very seriously. Finally, Napier wrote: "Some of the tracks are real. Sasquatch exists!"

This photograph was taken with a telephoto lens. It shows what appears to be a hairy, humanlike beast. The picture was taken in Spokane, Washington, on May 24, 1973. The photographer was 280 yards (256 m) away.

35

Minnesota Iceman

In 1968 an amazing story came to light. It was about a huge humanlike creature found in a block of ice.

In his book about Bigfoot and other creatures, John Napier said that Bigfoot existed. However, he also noted that some sightings were tricks. Among the cases that Napier listed as tricks was the case of the "Minnesota Iceman."

Ivan T. Sanderson and Bernard Heuvelmans were zoologists, or scientists who study animals. Sanderson had taken a great interest in stories of yeti and Bigfoot. Heuvelmans was particularly interested in sea creatures, such as the giant squid and the legendary sea serpent. On December 9, 1968, Sanderson received a telephone call from Terry Cullen, a snake salesman in Milwaukee. Cullen told Sanderson about a man named Frank Hansen. He had shown a strange, apelike creature at a Chicago livestock fair. It was frozen into a block of ice. Then he had traveled around the Midwest, showing it at carnivals.

Sanderson and Heuvelmans drove to Hansen's farm near Winona, Minnesota, on December 17. A trailer was parked near the farmhouse. Inside the trailer was a large freezer cabinet. It contained a large block of ice. Frozen in the ice was a creature that looked like a man covered with long brown hair.

This is a photograph of Frank Hansen's Minnesota Iceman (opposite). Was he a real creature, or just a clever trick?

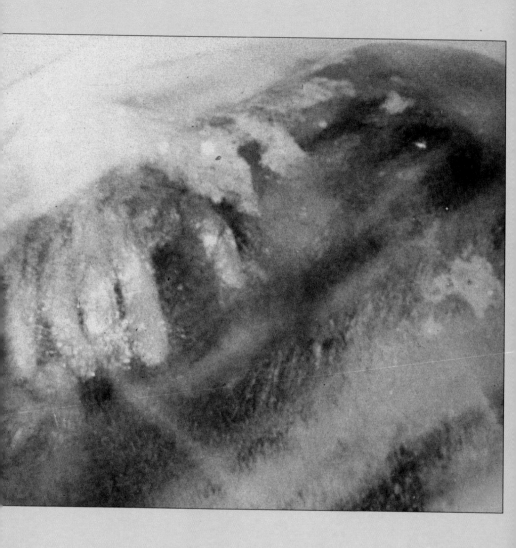

Hansen had shown a strange,
apelike creature at a Chicago
livestock fair. It was frozen
into a block of ice.

Hansen's freezer, containing the Iceman on public display in a shopping mall.

AN AMAZING FIND

Sanderson and Heuvelmans spent three days drawing and photographing the creature. The ice was thick, and in places it was covered with frost. Sanderson had to lie on top of the glass top of the freezer to draw the creature. It was difficult to take good photographs.

The creature had no hair on its face. It was male, and its left arm was thrown up above its head. In a report the scientists wrote that "the creature is somewhat pug-faced, the tip of the nose turning inward. The forehead is sloping. The mouth is slit-like."

But where had the creature come from? Hansen told various, confusing stories. At first, he said it had been found floating in a 6,000 pound (2,724 kg) block of ice off the coast of Siberia. Later, it had turned up in the warehouse of a salesman in Hong Kong. It was then bought by a millionaire who lived in California. Hansen would not give the name. He said he had borrowed the creature from the millionaire. A year later Hansen told a different tale. He said he had shot the creature in Minnesota in 1961.

However, Heuvelmans decided that the "Iceman" had survived from prehistory. He named the creature *Homo pongoides* ("apelike man"). The report appeared in a Belgian newspaper on March 19, 1969. Soon the news had traveled all over the world.

The Smithsonian Institution, in Washington D.C., wanted to see the creature, but Hansen said he had returned the Iceman to its millionaire owner. He claimed that his creature was just a model of the real one. Eventually, however, Hansen did let experts from the Smithsonian look in his freezer. The frost was cleared away and new photographs were taken.

NEANDERTHAL CONNECTION

Sanderson and the Smithsonian did further detective work. Three companies each claimed to have made a model for Hansen in 1967. Some years later, in 1981, a Rhode Island newspaper claimed that the figure had been made by a Disneyland artist named Howard Ball. Ball's widow said this was true.

The creature had no hair on its face. . . . its left arm was thrown up above its head.

Bernard Heuvelmans refused to believe this story. He was certain that the creature was a Neanderthal (*Homo sapiens neanderthalensis*), which were prehistoric humans. In 1974 Heuvelmans and Professor Boris Porschnev, who had studied the stories of other giant, hairy creatures called Almas, wrote a book together. Its title was *The Neanderthal Man Is Still Alive.*

Neanderthal Survivors?

In 1997 a scientist came up with a new idea. Could it connect prehistoric humans to the stories of giant, humanlike beasts?

Neanderthals were prehistoric humans. They were named after the Neander Valley, which is not far from Düsseldorf in Germany. This area is where the first remains of an ancient human-like skeleton were discovered in 1856. Since then more remains have been found in Europe, Asia, and along the North African coast.

Anthropologists are scientists who study the origin, history, customs, and beliefs of humans. They have worked out that Neanderthals lived about 200,000 to 30,000 years ago. Neanderthal skulls have thick browridges, large teeth, a huge jaw, and small cheekbones. They had powerful bodies, with large feet and hands.

DETECTIVE WORK

Until recently, anthropologists believed that the Neanderthals had gradually died out. They were followed by a different human species, the Cro-Magnons. Now, however, some experts have come up with a different idea. They believe it is possible that Neanderthals interbred with the Cro-Magnons some 30,000 years ago. In 1997, Professor Chris Stringer, from London's Natural History Museum, made an important suggestion

This head (opposite) shows what a Neanderthal woman might have looked like. The model was based on the measurements of a 41,000-year-old skull.

Until recently, anthropologists believed that the Neanderthals had gradually died out.

about DNA. DNA is a chemical found in the cells of every living thing. DNA is made of long strands. Sections of DNA, called genes, determine all of the physical characteristics of an individual. Specific genes in a certain order make a bird a bird and a human, human. Copies of genes are passed to offspring from their parents. This is why children often look like one or both of their parents or sometimes their grandparents. By comparing sections of DNA, an expert can trace genes from a child back to the mother and father and even earlier generations.

The prehistoric man . . . was a distant ancestor of the schoolteacher!

LIVING GENES

A few years ago researchers in England made an exciting discovery. They took DNA from the bones of a prehistoric man. Then they tried to find tiny pieces of matching DNA in people who still lived in the same area. They tested local schoolchildren, but they had no success. Then they tested the children's teacher. He had lived in the area all his life. There was no doubt. The prehistoric man who had lived there thousands of years before was a distant ancestor of the schoolteacher!

Professor Stringer had suggested that it might be possible to find traces of Neanderthal DNA in living people. This would prove that Neanderthals had not died out. Perhaps, he said, there are still such people living in wild, unexplored parts of the world.

Most reports of creatures, half-human and half-ape, come from eastern Asia. They cover the Himalayas, nearby southern China, and Mongolia. Even the frozen Minnesota Iceman may have come from there. According to one story told by Frank Hansen, who claimed that he had discovered the creature, the Minnesota Iceman had been found floating in a block of ice off the coast of Siberia.

ASIAN CONNECTIONS

In another of his stories of how he came across the beast, Hansen spoke of the body being found in a plastic bag. This was at the time of the Vietnam war, when the bodies of soldiers, sailors, and airmen were returned to the U.S. in "body bags." In November 1966, an article in the New York *World Journal Tribune* reported that Marines had been hunting in the thick forests. They shot tigers. "Other Marines," the article stated, "report that they shot a huge ape." But there are no known large apes in Vietnam, and

A forest in Vietnam. Some experts think that a Neanderthal might have walked from central Asia to Vietnam. There is, however, no proof of this.

although no Neanderthal bones have yet been found in Vietnam, it is possible that a surviving Neanderthal might have walked there from central Asia.

Was this the Iceman, and if so, was the creature a surviving Neanderthal? There are other facts to suggest that it might have been. One of the leaders of the Vietnamese National Liberation Front was Tran Dinh Minh. He told an Australian journalist about his experiences. One day he and some others saw tracks left by bare feet. They followed them and found a man sitting in a cave. He was covered with hair.

OTHER CONNECTIONS?

Strangely, there are still unusually hairy people living farther north, among the Japanese islands. These are called the Ainu. For hundreds of years the Ainu fought against the Japanese, until they were driven northward to the Hokkaido area. The Ainu have much more body hair than most other living human groups. Their language is unlike any other language.

However, most of the Ainu have now married people who are Japanese. There is no way of knowing what they once looked like. What is certain is that living Ainu do not look like Neanderthals.

But what about the North American Bigfoot? Could this be a Neanderthal?

Three Ainu fishermen in Japan. Ainu were once thought to be Neanderthal survivors.

This is a famous photograph. It shows the creature that François de Loys claimed to have killed in South America in 1917.

Millions of years ago all the continents of the world were joined together. Gradually the different pieces of land drifted apart. Even during the time of the Neanderthals, Alaska was still joined to Asia by a land bridge across the Bering Straits. Animals crossed over, and it is believed that Native Americans also came the same way. It is possible that some Neanderthals might have crossed over from Asia before them.

Around 1917 a scientific team led by Swiss scientist François de Loys was in the South American jungle—somewhere on the border of Colombia and Venezuela. They were attacked by apelike creatures and had to shoot one of them. Later they photographed the creature. It had a curiously humanlike face. It was over 5 feet (1.5 m) tall—much bigger than any known South American monkey. Later, in 1931, an Italian expedition collected stories people told about similar creatures.

BIGFOOT LIVES!

One scientist who believes that Bigfoot really exists is Grover Krantz, of Washington State University. His research into the creature began in 1969. He had soon collected more than 1,000 reports of sightings. Some people, he said, were "lying, were fooled by something else . . . or gave me information too poor to evaluate [decide one way or the other]. With the other half, I couldn't find anything wrong."

45

In June 1982, Paul Freeman was tracking a herd of elk near Walla Walla, Washington. Suddenly he saw a hairy figure about 60 yards (54 m) ahead. When it spotted him, the creature fled. Freeman found 21 clear footprints. He and Krantz made casts of them. Six days later they found another set of prints. Krantz decided they had been made by two different creatures. Both had feet about 15 inches (38 cm) long. The casts were so clear that he could see skin ridges (like fingerprints) on the soles of the feet. He said these would be impossible to fake. Since 1982 many more tracks have been found in the area.

NO REAL PROOF

So far nobody has produced a body—except the Minnesota Iceman, and that may be a trick. Some people who have seen Bigfoot say they did not want to shoot, because the creature appeared to be so human. So the mystery remains. Scientists such as Porshnev and Heuvelmans were sure that Neanderthals still lived. Many hunters have also been sure of what they saw. In wild areas of the world they claim to have seen and been watched by shy, hairy creatures. They move mostly at night, and they walk on two feet—like humans.

Grover Krantz (left) and Cliff Crook look at Bigfoot photographs at Bigfoot Central Headquarters in 1995.

Glossary

abominable Something that is unpleasant, below standard, or that causes great dislike. Abominable Snowman is the nickname of a giant humanlike beast said to live in the Himalayas.

academy A school that teaches a particular skill or subject. Also a group of experts working in the arts or sciences. For example, the Chinese Academy of Sciences.

advisors People who give other people, such as presidents and prime ministers, information or advice.

ancestor A member of the same family from a previous generation.

continent A great landmass such as Europe, Africa, or Asia.

descendant A member of a family following on from a previous generation of ancestors.

encounter A sudden, unexpected meeting with a person or thing.

examination Looking at something in detail. Also a task to test knowledge or ability.

exhausted Completely tired out, or something that has been completely used up.

expedition A trip or journey to find out about something.

footage An amount or length of film used in a camera.

genes Units that are inherited from parents which determine the characteristics of an offspring.

ice age A period of time when Earth was covered with ice.

ice ax A tool used to break up ice.

interbred Two different animal species that mate to produce young.

livestock Farm animals.

monastery A building where monks live and work.

Mongol A person from Mongolia, a country in East Central Asia.

plaster cast A copy of something made from plaster of paris, a quick-drying, chalky material that is mixed with water.

prehistoric A time before humans kept written historical records.

province An area within a country that makes its own rules and laws.

species A group of animals or plants that are similar and are able to mate and have offspring.

sprinter A person who runs short distances at high speed.

undergrowth Bushes, shrubs, and other low-lying plants.

zoologist A person who studies zoology, the science of animals.

Index

Further Reading

Bach, Julie S. *Bigfoot*, "Exploring the Unknown" series. Lucent Books, 1995

Coleman, Graham. *Neanderthal*. Gareth Stevens, 1996

Landau, Elaine. *Sasquatch, Wild Man of the Woods*, "Mysteries of Science" series. Millbrook Press, 1993

_____, _____. *Yeti, Abominable Snowman of the Himalayas*, "Mysteries of Science" series. Millbrook Press, 1993

Wayne, Kyra P. *Quest for Bigfoot*. Hancock House, 1996